VALUE OF TIME

AALEYAH RAHMANI

To those who seek meaning in every moment,
and understand that time is the most precious gift of all.

And to my family and friends,
whose presence makes every second worthwhile—
thank you for being my reason to value time.

Contents

Foreword

Time is the one resource we all share equally. Regardless of where we come from or who we are, each of us is given the same 24 hours in a day. Yet, how we use those hours defines the course of our lives.

In today's fast-paced world, it's easy to lose sight of the value of time. We fill our days with endless tasks, distractions, and responsibilities, often forgetting that every moment we spend is a moment we'll never get back. This book is a heartfelt reminder of time's importance—a gentle nudge to slow down, reflect, and make intentional choices.

Through its pages, you'll find insights, stories, and inspiration designed to help you see time not just as a fleeting resource but as a priceless gift. Whether you're seeking more purpose in your daily routine, striving to accomplish your dreams, or simply hoping to savor the present moment, this book will guide you on that journey.

It's not just a book about managing time; it's about appreciating it. The lessons within are universal and timeless, just like the subject itself.

So, as you read these pages, I hope you'll pause, reflect, and perhaps even reimagine how you spend the most valuable currency you'll ever own—your time.

Preface

Time has always fascinated me. It moves steadily forward, indifferent to our desires, yet it shapes every aspect of our lives. We often take it for granted, spending hours on trivial pursuits while yearning for more of it when faced with life's most precious moments. This paradox inspired me to write this book.

In a world filled with distractions, the importance of time has never been more critical. We are constantly juggling responsibilities, ambitions, and relationships, often forgetting that every tick of the clock brings us closer to the fleeting nature of existence. This book is my attempt to highlight the profound value of time—not as a burden, but as an opportunity.

With the help of thoughtful insights and meaningful reflections, I hope to guide readers toward a deeper appreciation for the moments that make up their lives. This book is not about how to do more in less time or become more efficient; it's about making time meaningful.

Writing this book has been a journey of introspection and discovery for me, and I hope it will spark the same sense of purpose in you. Time is precious, not because it's finite, but because it holds the potential for growth, connection, and joy.

Thank you for taking the time to read this book. I hope it inspires you to value your moments and create a life filled with intention and fulfillment.

- Aaleyah Rahmani

Acknowledgements

Writing this book has been an incredible journey, and I would not have been able to complete it without the support and encouragement of many wonderful people.

To my family, thank you for your unwavering belief in me and for reminding me of the importance of spending time with loved ones. Your love and support have been my greatest source of strength and inspiration.

To my teachers, who have shared their knowledge, guidance, and wisdom with me, your influence has been invaluable. Thank you for shaping my understanding and for inspiring me to think deeply about life's most important lessons.

Finally, to you, the reader, thank you for choosing to spend your valuable time with this book. I hope its words resonate with you and inspire you to embrace the beauty and potential of every moment.

This book is a testament to the truth that none of us can walk this path alone. It is with deep gratitude that I acknowledge everyone who has made this work possible.

Prologue

Time is the one thing we can never get back. It slips through our fingers, often unnoticed, until we realize it's gone. In a world where everything moves faster, where distractions are constant, and where the pressures of modern life never seem to stop, it becomes easy to lose sight of time's true value.

Yet, the way we spend our time shapes our lives. Every decision, every moment, every choice we make is influenced by how we use time. This book is an invitation to slow down and reconsider the way we approach the passing hours. It is a reminder that time, though fleeting, holds the power to change everything—if we understand its worth.

In these pages, you'll discover not just the importance of time, but how to make the most of it. You'll learn that time isn't just something to manage, but something to cherish.

The journey ahead is not one of finding more hours in the day, but of learning how to live with purpose and intention in the hours you already have.

CHAPTER ONE

The Currency of Life

Opening Thought

"Imagine you had a bank account that gave you 86,400 seconds every morning. And at the end of the day, whatever you didn't spend is just gone. No rollovers. No refunds. How would you spend your time?"

Time: Our Most Valuable Resource

Time is one of those things we all know is important, but we don't always treat it like it is. We say, "I don't have time" when we're busy, but the truth is, we all have the same 24 hours each day. It's just a matter of how we choose to use them. Unlike money, time doesn't grow on trees. It's not something you can save up for a rainy day or buy back once it's gone. Every single day, you get 86,400 seconds. And once they're gone, that's it. You don't get them back.

The Reality of Time

We all have the same amount of time, yet we can't seem to agree on how to use it. The richest person in the world can't buy more hours, just like the busiest person can't make time stretch longer. We're all limited by the same thing: time. Sometimes it feels like there's never enough, and other times it feels like it's just slipping away, especially when we're distracted. But no matter what, it keeps moving forward.

The Cost of Time

Every time we spend a moment doing one thing, we're choosing not to do something else. When you scroll through your phone for an hour, you're not spending that time with your family, or on a hobby, or resting. You're choosing to spend it in one way—and that's the thing about time—it's always moving, and every second is a choice. We don't always see the cost of those small moments until later. You can always make more money, but you can't make more time. That hour you spent scrolling through your feed? That's gone, and it doesn't come back. The question is, did it give you something that was worth it?

The Paradox of Time

Here's where it gets interesting. Sometimes, when we're busy, it feels like time is moving too fast. You blink and a whole day has passed. But then, on the rare occasions when we're just relaxing or doing something we really enjoy, time seems to stretch. That afternoon you spend reading or chatting with a friend—it feels like it lasts forever, even though it's only a few hours. This is the paradox of time: it moves the same for everyone, but it feels different depending on how we're experiencing it. When we're anxious or rushing, it seems like time's slipping away. But when we're present, when we're in the moment, it feels like there's plenty of it.

Time Reveals What Matters

If you really think about it, how you spend your time says a lot about what's important to you. We often tell ourselves we don't have enough time for things like exercise, family, or pursuing our passions—but the truth is, we make time for the things that matter most. Whether that's work, Netflix, or social media—it's all a choice. And it's not just about what you want to do, it's about what you're willing to prioritize. Look at your calendar. What does it say about where you're investing your time? Does it align with what you value most? If not, why not? We're all busy, but at the end of the day, how we spend our time is what shapes our lives.

Reclaiming Your Time

The good news? Time is something you can take control of. It's about making choices. It's about deciding what's important to you and making time for it. And it's not about being perfect or squeezing every second out of the day—it's about being intentional with the moments you have. Time doesn't slow down for anyone, but we can slow down and choose how to spend it. The key is realizing that time is a gift. And how you use it will determine the kind of life you build. It's all in how you spend it.

Closing Thought

"What would it be like if you treated your time like the precious resource it is? How would your days change if you really thought about how you're using every moment?"

CHAPTER TWO

Mastering Time: How to Manage What Matters

Time Management: It's About Making Smart Choices
When people talk about time management, they often think it means having a super strict schedule with every minute planned out. But that's not really the case. Time management is just about being smart with how you use your time. It's about figuring out what matters most to you, and making sure you spend your time on those things, not just on whatever pops up. You don't have to be busy all the time to manage your time well. What matters is what you choose to focus on.

Learning to Say "No"
One of the hardest parts about managing time is learning to say "no." A lot of people, especially your friends or family, might ask you to do things. And it's hard to say no, right? You don't want to let anyone down. But here's the thing: every time you say "yes" to something, you might be saying "no" to something that's more important to you. For example, if you say "yes" to hanging out with friends when you really need to finish a homework assignment, you're saying no to your schoolwork and your future goals. It's okay to say "no" sometimes—it helps you protect your time for what really matters.

Focus on What's Important, Not Just What's Urgent
It's easy to get distracted by things that seem important right now—like responding to a text or checking social media. But just because something seems urgent, like a notification popping up, doesn't mean it's the best use of your time. The real key to time management is learning to spend your time on things that are important, not just urgent. Things that are important will help you reach your bigger goals, like doing well in school or practicing a hobby you care about. Urgent things might be small tasks, but they won't

always help you get closer to your dreams.

The Power of Priorities

Take a minute and think about what's important to you. What do you care about the most? Maybe it's school, sports, family, or learning a new skill. Whatever it is, when you know what matters most, you can spend more time on those things. For example, if your goal is to get better at a sport, you might decide that practicing every day is a priority. If you know that, you'll make sure to set aside time for practice, instead of getting distracted by things that aren't as important.

Small Changes Can Make a Big Difference

You don't have to make huge changes to manage your time better. Even little things can make a big difference. Here are a few easy ideas: Start your day by doing the one thing that will make you feel good, like finishing your homework or working on something you love. Break big tasks into smaller ones so you don't feel overwhelmed. For example, instead of saying, "I have to study for the whole exam," try, "I'm going to study this chapter first." Take short breaks when you're working. Resting for a few minutes can help you feel more focused and energized. These small shifts can make your days feel less stressful and more balanced.

Make Time for What's Really Important

Good time management isn't just about getting everything done—it's also about making sure you have time for yourself. This includes relaxing, hanging out with friends, or doing things you love. Don't let your whole day be filled with work or school stuff. It's important to take care of your mind and body by having fun and resting too.

The Balance Between Planning and Flexibility

Sometimes things don't go according to plan. Maybe you had a plan for the day, but then something unexpected comes up. That's okay! The key is to stay flexible. You can make a plan for how you want to spend your time, but also be ready to adjust if things change. If something doesn't go as planned, don't stress out. Just roll with it and get back on track when you can. Flexibility is just as important as having a plan.

Closing Reflection

"Imagine if you spent more of your time doing the things that really matter to you. What would your day look like if you focused more on the important things and less on the small, distracting stuff?"

Exercise

Think about your day and write down three things you want to spend more time on. What are they? Maybe it's spending more time with family, focusing more on school, or practicing a hobby. Now, look at your calendar or to-do list. Are there things you can say no to, so you can make room for what matters most?

Summary of Key Points

Time management isn't about being busy all the time—it's about making smart choices. Saying "no" is okay. It helps you focus on the important things. Focus on what's important to you, not just what feels urgent. Small changes can make your days feel less stressful. Make time for fun and relaxation, not just work. Be flexible. Things don't always go as planned, and that's okay!

CHAPTER THREE

Time and Focus: The Power of Being Present

In this chapter, we're going to talk about something that can make your time more useful and even more enjoyable: focus. It sounds simple, but focusing on what you're doing right now is one of the best ways to get more done and feel less stressed.

It's super easy to get distracted these days. Between social media, games, messages, and everything else, our brains can feel like they're bouncing from one thing to another. But here's the thing: when you focus on one task at a time, you do it better and faster. You also don't feel as overwhelmed.

For example, imagine you're doing homework. If you keep checking your phone, it might take you longer to finish your work because you keep getting distracted. But if you focus only on your homework, you'll probably get it done quicker and feel proud of your work.

Being present is about not thinking about what you're doing next or worrying about something that happened earlier. It means giving all your attention to the task in front of you. If you focus on what you're doing right now, you'll do a better job and feel more satisfied with how your time was spent.

Now, you might think, "But I can do more things if I multitask, right?" Actually, multitasking can make things take longer. When you switch between tasks, like checking a text message and then going back to your homework, it can slow you down because your brain has to catch up. It's way better to focus on one thing at a time and do it well.

Here are a few ways to stay focused and be more present:

Put your phone away or on silent: When you're working on something important, like studying or reading, try to keep your phone out of sight. It's way easier to focus without distractions.

Use a timer: Try working for 20 or 30 minutes straight and then take a short break. This can help you stay on track. It's called the Pomodoro technique, and it helps a lot with focus.

Take breaks: You don't have to work nonstop. Give yourself breaks to rest, even for just 5 minutes. Taking breaks helps you recharge and keep your mind fresh.

Practice being mindful: Mindfulness is when you pay close attention to what you're doing right now, without thinking about anything else. You can practice this while doing anything—like walking, eating, or even just sitting still for a few minutes. It helps your brain stay calm and focused.

The more you practice these things, the easier it will get to focus on one task at a time. And when you focus better, you'll actually get more done and feel less stressed.

But remember, it's also important to make time for fun and relaxation. Being present doesn't mean you can't enjoy life. Take time to hang out with friends, play games, or just chill. Those moments will help you feel more balanced and ready to focus when you need to.

Time is precious, and being focused makes the most of it. If you spend more time paying attention to what you're doing right now, you'll find that you're able to get things done faster, feel more satisfied, and enjoy your time more.

CHAPTER FOUR

Time and Energy: How to Use Both Wisely

In this chapter, we're going to talk about how time and energy are connected. You might not realize it, but how you use your energy is just as important as how you use your time. Sometimes, it's not just about how much time you have, but how much energy you have to spend in that time.

Have you ever tried to do something important when you're super tired, and it feels impossible? Or maybe you've tried to study or finish a project, but your mind keeps wandering, and you don't feel motivated? That's because your energy affects your ability to focus and get things done.

So, how can we make sure we're using both time and energy wisely? Here are some tips to help you manage both.

1. Know Your Energy Levels

Everyone has certain times of the day when they feel most awake and focused. For some people, it's in the morning, right after they wake up. For others, it might be in the afternoon or even late at night. Take note of when you feel most energetic and use that time to do your most important work, like studying, practicing a hobby, or tackling tough tasks.

If you try to do hard work when you're already feeling tired, it'll be harder and take more time. But if you do it when you're feeling alert and ready, you'll get it done faster and feel better about it.

2. Take Care of Your Body

If you want to have the energy to do things you enjoy or need to get done, you have to take care of your body. That means getting enough sleep, eating good food, and staying active. When your body is well-rested and healthy, your mind is sharper and you can get more done.

Sleep is super important for energy. If you don't get enough sleep, you might feel groggy or sluggish the next day, and it's hard to focus. Try to get at least 8 hours of sleep, especially if you have school or something important the next day.

Eating healthy foods gives you the fuel you need to stay active and focused. Eating too much junk food can leave you feeling tired or distracted. So, try to eat a mix of fruits, vegetables, proteins, and whole grains for better energy.

3. Take Breaks

Even if you're feeling super focused, your brain and body can get tired after a while. Taking short breaks gives you a chance to rest and recharge. It's like giving your brain a little vacation. If you study or work for too long without a break, you'll start to feel exhausted, and it'll take you longer to finish tasks.

Try working for 25-30 minutes and then take a 5-minute break. You can stretch, grab a snack, or just relax. After a few rounds of this, take a longer break, like 15 minutes. This helps keep your energy high and your brain sharp.

4. Don't Overload Yourself

It's easy to get excited about doing lots of things, but trying to do everything at once can drain your energy really fast. It's important to know your limits and not overfill your schedule. If you've got a lot going on, it's okay to say "no" to some things or ask for help. You don't have to do everything by yourself.

When you focus on a few important things, you can do them better. Spreading yourself too thin makes it harder to give your best effort. So, choose a few things that really matter, and give them your full energy.

5. Find Time to Relax

It's important to give your brain and body time to relax and have fun. Don't spend all your time working or studying. If you're always on the go, you'll eventually burn out. Find time to relax, do something you enjoy, or hang out with friends. Doing things that make you happy helps you recharge your energy, so you can be even more focused when you're working.

Remember, having fun and relaxing is just as important as working hard. Balance is key.

Closing Thoughts

Managing your energy is a big part of managing your time. When you use your energy wisely, you'll get more out of the time you have. Make sure to rest, eat well, take breaks, and use your most energetic hours for the most important tasks. By doing this, you'll feel more focused, less stressed, and ready to tackle whatever comes your way.

Exercise

Think about the times when you feel most energetic. Do you feel better in the morning, afternoon, or evening? Write down your answers and see if you can plan your day to do your most important tasks during those times. Also, think about how you can take better care of your body to feel more energized—maybe getting more sleep, eating healthier, or taking more breaks.

CHAPTER FIVE

Time and Goals: How to Set Goals and Make Time for Them

In this chapter, we're going to talk about how to use your time wisely to achieve your goals. We all have dreams and things we want to accomplish, but sometimes it can be hard to figure out how to make those things happen. The key is setting clear goals and using your time to work toward them.

1. What Are Goals?

Goals are things you want to achieve. They could be big, like becoming good at a sport or getting good grades in school. Or they could be smaller, like learning a new hobby or finishing a project. Goals help you focus on what's important, and they give you something to work toward.

Without goals, it's easy to waste time or feel lost. But when you have a goal in mind, you know exactly what you're working for, which makes it easier to make choices about how to spend your time.

2. How to Set Good Goals

Not all goals are the same. If you want to achieve something, you need to make sure your goals are clear, specific, and realistic. Here's how you can do that:

Make it specific: Instead of saying, "I want to be better at school," say, "I want to get an A on my next math test." Being specific helps you know exactly what you need to do.

Make it measurable: This means you should be able to track your progress. For example, if your goal is to read more books, set a goal like, "I will read one book every month." That way, you can measure how much you're improving.

Make it realistic: Make sure your goal is something you can actually achieve. Don't make a goal that's too big to reach right now. It's okay to start small and work your way up.

Give yourself a timeline: Set a deadline for your goal. If you don't have a timeline, it's easy to put things off. For example, instead of saying, "I'll finish my project sometime," say, "I'll finish my project by next Friday."

3. Making Time for Your Goals

Once you've set your goals, the next step is to make time for them. It's easy to get busy with other things and forget about what's really important. To make time for your goals, you need to prioritize them.

Here's how you can do that:

Plan your time: Look at your week and decide when you will work on your goals. Maybe you set aside 30 minutes every day after school to study or practice your hobby. Make time for your goals just like you make time for other things.

Break big goals into smaller steps: If your goal feels too big, break it down into smaller, easier steps. For example, if your goal is to write a book (like the one you're working on!), break it down into smaller tasks like, "Write one chapter a week" or "Write for 30 minutes every day."

Avoid distractions: When you're working on your goal, try to focus. Put away your phone, turn off the TV, and give yourself time to focus fully on what you're trying to achieve.

4. Stay Motivated

Working on goals can be tough, especially if they take time. Sometimes it can feel like you're not making progress, or you might want to quit. But the key is to keep going, even when it feels hard. Here are a few ways to stay motivated:

Track your progress: Seeing how far you've come can keep you motivated. Keep a record of your achievements, even the small ones. This will remind you that you're making progress.

Celebrate small wins: Every time you achieve a little part of your goal, take a moment to celebrate. If you finished a chapter of your book or got a good grade on a test, give yourself a reward like watching your favorite show or eating a treat.

Remember why you started: Think about why you wanted to achieve your goal in the first place. Keeping that in mind will help you push through the tough times.

5. Don't Be Afraid to Adjust Your Goals

Sometimes, things don't go as planned. Maybe something unexpected happens, or you realize your goal isn't exactly what you want anymore. That's okay! It's important to be flexible and adjust your goals when needed. Just because you set a goal doesn't mean you can't change it if it's no longer working for you.

Closing Thoughts

Goals give you something to work toward, and making time for them is one of the best ways to use your time wisely. By setting clear, realistic goals, breaking them into smaller steps, and staying motivated, you can achieve anything you set your mind to. And remember, it's okay to adjust your goals if needed. The most important thing is to keep moving forward, one step at a time.

Exercise

Write down one goal you want to achieve in the next month. It could be anything! Maybe you want to improve in a sport, get better at a subject in school, or start a new hobby. Break that goal down into smaller steps and think about when you can work on it during the week. Track your progress and celebrate your wins !!

CHAPTER SIX

Time and Habits: How Small Changes Add Up

In this chapter, we're going to talk about how your habits can affect your time. You might not realize it, but the little things you do every day can add up to make a big difference in how you use your time. Good habits can help you use your time more wisely, while bad habits can waste it.

1. What Are Habits?

Habits are things you do regularly, almost without thinking about them. Some habits are good, like brushing your teeth every morning or doing your homework on time. Other habits might not be as helpful, like spending too much time on your phone or leaving things until the last minute.

The best part about habits is that they are powerful. When you develop a good habit, it can make your life easier and save you time. But bad habits can take up your time and energy without you even noticing.

2. How to Build Good Habits

Building a good habit might seem hard at first, but with some practice, it becomes easier. Here are some steps to help you develop good habits:

Start small: Trying to change everything at once can be overwhelming. Start with one small habit. For example, if you want to read more, start by reading just 10 minutes a day instead of hours. Once that becomes a habit, you can increase it over time.

Be consistent: The key to building a habit is doing it regularly. Even if it's just for a few minutes, try to do your new habit every day. Consistency is what makes a habit stick.

Track your progress: Keep track of your habit with a journal or a habit tracker. Every time you do it, check it off. This gives you something to look back on and see how much progress you've made.

Reward yourself: Give yourself a little reward when you stick to your habit. For example, if you work out for a week straight, treat yourself to something you enjoy.

3. How to Break Bad Habits

Just as good habits can help you use your time better, bad habits can waste your time. If you spend hours on your phone or put off important tasks until the last minute, these habits can make you feel stressed and disorganized.

The good news is that you can break bad habits, but it takes time and effort. Here's how you can do it:

Recognize the habit: The first step in breaking a bad habit is noticing when you do it. For example, if you tend to procrastinate, ask yourself why you're putting something off. Is it because it's hard or boring? Once you understand why you do it, you can work on changing it.

Replace it with something better: It's easier to replace a bad habit with a good one than to just stop doing something. If you tend to waste time on your phone, replace it with something productive, like reading or exercising. Over time, your new habit will become just as automatic as the old one.

Be patient with yourself: Breaking bad habits isn't easy, and it can take time. Don't be too hard on yourself if you slip up. Keep trying, and soon enough, the old habit will fade away.

4. How to Make Your Day More Productive with Habits

When you have good habits, your day becomes smoother and more productive. Here are a few habits that can help you make the most of your time:

Plan your day the night before: Spend a few minutes each evening planning what you want to do the next day. This will help you stay organized and use your time wisely.

Use a morning routine: Starting your day with a morning routine can set the tone for the rest of the day. Whether it's stretching, reading, or eating a healthy breakfast, having a routine can make you feel more energized and ready to go.

Take breaks throughout the day: Just like we talked about earlier, taking breaks can help keep your mind fresh. Make it a habit to take short breaks during long tasks to keep your energy up.

5. The Power of Small Changes

The amazing thing about habits is that small changes add up over time. If you spend just 10 minutes a day doing something productive, like practicing an instrument or writing, that adds up to over an hour each week! If you spend that time on something important to you, you'll be amazed at how much you can accomplish.

The same goes for bad habits. If you spend 30 minutes a day on something that doesn't really matter, like scrolling through social media, that adds up to over 3 hours a week. That's time you could be using for something better, like working on a goal, reading, or learning something new.

Closing Thoughts

The habits you build every day play a big part in how you use your time. Whether they are good habits or bad habits, they all add up over time. By focusing on building good habits and breaking the ones that waste your time, you can make the most of every day. Remember, small changes can lead to big results!

Exercise

Think about one habit you want to build (like reading every day or exercising). Write down one small step you can take to get started today. Also, pick one bad habit you want to break and think about a better habit you can replace it with. Start with small changes, and you'll see big results over time!

CHAPTER SEVEN

Time and Reflection: Why Taking Time to Think Helps You Grow

There are many ways to reflect on your time, but here are a few simple ways to get started:

Keep a journal: Journaling is one of the best ways to reflect. You can write down what you did each day and how you felt about it. At the end of the week, you can look back and see what worked well and what didn't.

Ask yourself questions: At the end of each day or week, ask yourself some simple questions like:

What did I accomplish today?

How did I feel during my day?

Did I use my time wisely?

What could I improve next time?

Set aside time to think: You doIn this chapter, we're going to talk about something really important that many people overlook—reflection. Reflection means taking time to think about your actions, how you spend your time, and what you've learned from experiences. It might sound like a lot of work, but reflecting on your time can help you make better choices and improve your life.

1. What Is Reflection?

Reflection is when you stop and think about what's happened in your life. It's looking back at your day, week, or even year, and asking yourself questions like:

What did I do today?

What went well?

What didn't go as planned?

How did I spend my time?

What can I do differently next time?

By reflecting, you can learn from your experiences, figure out what's working for you, and what's not. It's a way of using your time in a deeper way. Instead of just moving through life without thinking about it, you take a moment to understand how you're spending your time, and that can help you make better decisions going forward.

2. Why Is Reflection Important?

You might wonder why reflecting is important, especially if you're already busy. Well, reflection helps you:

Learn from mistakes: We all make mistakes. Reflection helps you understand why something didn't work out, so you can avoid making the same mistake again.

Celebrate successes: It's easy to forget your achievements, especially when you're busy. But taking time to reflect on your successes, big or small, can help you feel proud and motivated.

Plan for the future: Reflecting on your time helps you set better goals for the future. If you look at how you spent your time last month, you can decide what changes you want to make next month.

3. How to Reflect on Your Time

don't need to write anything down if you don't want to. Sometimes, just sitting in a quiet place and thinking about your day or week can help you figure out what's important.

4. Reflection and Growth

One of the best things about reflection is that it helps you grow. When you look back at how you've spent your time, you can see where you've improved and where you can do better. This helps you get better over time.

For example, if you notice that you've been wasting a lot of time on your phone, you can decide to spend less time on it and focus more on your goals. If you've been spending a lot of time with friends or family, you can reflect on how those moments made you feel and how they're helping you grow as a person.

Reflection also helps you celebrate your growth. You might not notice how much you're improving every day, but if you look back over time, you'll see that you've learned a lot and made progress.

5. Reflection and Time Management

Reflection is also a great tool for time management. By reflecting on how you use your time, you can see where you might be wasting it or where you could use it better. Maybe you're spending too much time on things that don't matter, or you're getting distracted by things that take up your energy without giving you anything in return.

Reflection can help you:

Identify where you're wasting time: If you reflect on how you spent your time, you might notice that you're spending too much time on social media or watching TV. Once you realize that, you can decide to spend that time more wisely, like working on your goals or learning something new.

Make better decisions: If you take time to reflect on your choices, you'll be able to make better ones in the future. For example, you might reflect on a time when you didn't study enough and ended up with a bad grade. Next time, you'll remember how important studying is and plan your time better.

Closing Thoughts

Reflection is like looking in a mirror, but for your life. It helps you see where you've been, where you are, and where you're going. By reflecting on your time and experiences, you can learn from them, celebrate your wins, and make better decisions for the future.

Don't be afraid to spend time thinking about how you use your time. The more you reflect, the more you'll understand yourself and how you can make the best of every moment.

Exercise

At the end of this week, take a few minutes to reflect on how you spent your time. What went well? What could you do better next week? Write down your thoughts and think about one small change you can make to use your time more wisely.

CHAPTER EIGHT

Time and Distractions: How to Stay Focused

In today's world, distractions are everywhere. Whether it's social media, video games, texting, or even just random thoughts popping into your head, staying focused can be really tough. But the truth is, distractions can eat up a lot of your time, and the more you give into them, the less time you have for things that matter.

In this chapter, we'll explore how distractions affect your time and how you can fight back to stay focused on your goals.

1. What Are Distractions?

Distractions are anything that takes your attention away from what you should be doing. It could be a notification on your phone, your friends talking to you, or even just daydreaming. Distractions make it hard to concentrate, and when you're distracted, you're not using your time in the best way possible.

We all get distracted from time to time, but the important thing is learning how to manage distractions so they don't waste your time. The longer you stay distracted, the harder it is to get back on track. That's why it's important to understand what causes distractions and how you can deal with them.

2. Why Are Distractions So Hard to Resist?

It's easy to give in to distractions because they often feel rewarding in the moment. When you check your phone or watch a funny video, it feels good and can give you a quick burst of happiness. But the problem is, these distractions often take up more time than we realize. Before you know it, you've spent hours on things that don't help you get closer to your goals.

The reason distractions are so hard to resist is that they feel more immediate than the work you need to do. You might have a long-term goal, like finishing a project or studying for a test, but those tasks often don't give you immediate rewards like a funny meme or a game.

3. How to Recognize Distractions

The first step in dealing with distractions is to recognize them. Ask yourself, "What is taking my attention away from what I'm supposed to be doing?" Is it your phone, TV, or a conversation with a friend? Or maybe you're just feeling bored, and your mind starts to wander.

Sometimes distractions aren't just external—they can also be internal, like worrying about something or feeling overwhelmed. You might start thinking, "I'm never going to finish this work," or "I don't feel like doing this right now." These thoughts can distract you just as much as anything around you.

4. How to Avoid Distractions

Here are some ways you can avoid distractions and stay focused on what you need to do:

Turn off notifications: One of the biggest distractions today is your phone. Notifications from social media, messages, or apps can pull you away from what you're working on. Try turning off notifications while you work or study so you're not tempted to check your phone every few minutes.

Create a distraction-free zone: Set up a place where you can work without being interrupted. This could be your room, a quiet corner, or a study spot. Keep this space clear of anything that might distract you, like your phone, TV, or toys. If you need to, put on headphones or play music that helps you focus.

Set time limits for distractions: If you know you're going to get distracted, set a time limit for when you can check your phone or take a break. For example, you could work for 30 minutes and then allow yourself a 5-minute break to check your messages. This way, you get your work done but still give yourself a little reward.

Use the "Pomodoro" Technique: This technique involves working in short bursts. You work for 25 minutes, then take a 5-minute break. After four sessions, you take a longer break. This method helps you stay focused and avoid burnout. Plus, knowing that a break is coming soon makes it easier to stay on track.

5. How to Get Back on Track After a Distraction

Sometimes, even when we try to avoid distractions, we get pulled away from our work. It's okay—it happens to everyone. The key is to not let it completely throw you off track. Here's what you can do to get back on track:

Acknowledge the distraction: If you get distracted, don't beat yourself up about it. Just notice what happened and move on. Don't waste time feeling guilty or frustrated—it won't help you focus.

Refocus on your task: Once you realize you've been distracted, take a deep breath and go back to the task at hand. Remember your goal and remind yourself why you're working in the first place.

Use a timer: If you find yourself getting distracted a lot, set a timer for a specific amount of time to work. Knowing you have a set time to focus can help you stay committed and avoid distractions.

6. The Power of Breaks

When you're working hard and staying focused, it's important to take breaks. But these breaks should be planned and not turn into distractions. When you take a break, try to do something that helps you recharge, like stretching, grabbing a snack, or taking a walk.

Taking breaks is important because it helps you avoid mental burnout. Working for long periods without a break can make you tired and less focused. So, even though it might feel like you're wasting time, taking short breaks actually helps you be more productive.

Closing Thoughts

Distractions are everywhere, but learning how to deal with them is one of the best ways to make the most of your time. By creating a distraction-free environment, using time management techniques, and staying focused, you can make sure you're using your time in the best way possible.

Remember, it's not about completely avoiding distractions—it's about finding a balance. Give yourself time to relax and enjoy things, but also make sure you're staying focused when you need to.

Exercise

Think about a time when you got distracted and lost track of time. What was the distraction? Next time you're working, try to notice when you get distracted. Write down your plan for how you can avoid or deal with that distraction. Try to stay focused for a set amount of time and give yourself a reward afterward.

CHAPTER NINE

Time and Relationships: Balancing People with Productivity

As you go through life, one of the most important things you'll have to figure out is how to balance your time with the people you care about—family, friends, and other loved ones—while still being productive and working on your goals. Time with the people you love is precious, and it's just as important as spending time on your schoolwork, hobbies, or other goals. But it can sometimes feel like there's just not enough time for both.

In this chapter, we'll talk about how you can balance spending time with others while still making sure you have time for your responsibilities and dreams.

1. Why Relationships Matter

People are one of the most important parts of life. Whether it's your family, friends, or other loved ones, these relationships give you support, joy, and memories. Spending time with people you care about can make you feel happier and less stressed. It can also help you grow as a person, because relationships teach you important life lessons.

At the same time, you also have your personal goals and responsibilities that require time and focus. So, how do you balance spending time with others and getting your work done? The answer is time management and setting priorities.

2. Setting Priorities: What Comes First?

One of the first steps in balancing your time is deciding what's most important. Sometimes, life can be overwhelming, and you might feel like you have to choose between hanging out with your friends or getting your homework done. The key is to set your priorities and manage your time wisely.

Here's how you can figure out what comes first:

Understand what matters most to you: Is your homework deadline coming up? Do you have an important event or celebration with family or friends? Figure out what needs your attention right now. When you know what's most important, it's easier to make decisions about how to spend your time.

Be honest about your time: If you know you have something important to do, don't overcommit to plans that might take up too much of your time. If you need to study for an exam, you can explain to your friends that you need to focus for a while but that you'll catch up with them later.

Use a schedule: A schedule can help you balance your time between people and productivity. Set aside specific times for studying, working on your goals, and spending time with family and friends. A schedule helps you see exactly where your time is going, so you can make sure you're giving enough attention to both work and relationships.

3. Making Time for People Without Sacrificing Your Goals

It's easy to get caught up in work and forget to spend time with people. But relationships need time, too. Here are some ways to make sure you're giving both people and productivity the time they deserve:

Be intentional with your time: When you're with someone, really focus on being with them. Put away your phone, stop checking your messages, and give them your full attention. When you do this, even short moments can feel special and meaningful.

Use your breaks wisely: You don't need to spend hours with people to enjoy their company. If you're studying or working on a project, use your breaks to connect with someone. You could take a quick walk with a friend or chat with your family over lunch. These small moments add up and help you stay connected.

Involve people in your goals: You don't always have to separate time for people from time for your goals. Sometimes, you can combine them. For example, if you're working on a hobby or project, invite a friend or family member to join you. This way, you can be productive and enjoy quality time together.

4. Learning to Say "No"

As you try to balance your time, there will be moments when you have to say "no" to something. Saying no isn't always easy, especially if you don't want to disappoint someone. But learning to say no can help you protect your time and energy for the things that matter most.

Here's how you can say no respectfully:

Be honest: If someone invites you to hang out but you have work to do, it's okay to say no. You can explain that you have an important task and that you'll catch up with them later. People will appreciate your honesty.

Offer an alternative: If you're busy but still want to spend time with someone, suggest a different time. For example, "I can't hang out right now because I have homework, but how about we meet up this weekend?"

5. Quality Time Over Quantity

Sometimes, it's not about how much time you spend with someone, but how you spend that time. You don't need to spend hours hanging out or talking to show you care. It's about making the time you do have meaningful.

For example:

Family dinners: Even if it's just a short dinner together, sitting down as a family without distractions can help you connect and enjoy each other's company.

Short chats with friends: A quick call or message can go a long way in maintaining a friendship, even if you can't hang out in person.

Remember, quality time is about being present. When you give someone your full attention, even a small amount of time can feel special.

6. Don't Forget About Yourself

When you're balancing time with others and your goals, it's easy to forget about your own needs. You might be busy trying to make everyone else happy, but it's also important to take care of yourself. Make sure you're finding time to relax, recharge, and enjoy the things you love.

This will help you stay healthy, energized, and ready to manage your time for both people and productivity.

Closing Thoughts

Balancing time with people and being productive isn't always easy, but with the right time management skills, it's possible. By setting priorities, making intentional time for relationships, and managing your schedule, you can make sure you're giving both people and your goals the attention they deserve. And remember, it's not about spending all your time with others or all your time on work. It's about finding a balance that works for you and helps you grow.

Exercise

Think about how you spend your time with family and friends versus how much time you spend on your goals or work. Are you balancing both well? Write down one way you can spend more quality time with someone you care about without sacrificing your responsibilities. Also, think of a situation where you need to say "no" to something to make room for what matters more.

CHAPTER TEN

Time and Mindset: How Your Thoughts Shape Your Time

In this final chapter, we're going to talk about something that might seem a bit different from what we've covered so far: your mindset. Your mindset, or the way you think about time and life, plays a huge role in how you actually use your time. If you have a positive and growth-oriented mindset, you're much more likely to use your time wisely and achieve your goals. On the other hand, a negative mindset can hold you back and make it harder to manage your time well.

In this chapter, we'll explore how your mindset affects your time and how you can develop a mindset that helps you make the most of every moment.

1. What Is Mindset and Why Does It Matter?

Mindset is the way you think about yourself, your abilities, and the world around you. There are two main types of mindsets that can affect how you spend your time:

Fixed mindset: A fixed mindset is when you believe that your abilities and intelligence are set in stone. You might think things like, "I'm just not good at math," or "I'll never be able to learn that." People with a fixed mindset often avoid challenges because they fear failure.

Growth mindset: A growth mindset is when you believe that you can improve with effort and practice. You might think, "I might not be good at this now, but I can get better if I keep trying." People with a growth mindset embrace challenges and see failure as an opportunity to learn and grow.

Your mindset affects how you spend your time because if you believe you can improve, you're more likely to put in the effort and use your time wisely. If you think you can't change or grow, you might give up too easily or waste time because you don't believe it will make a difference.

2. How a Growth Mindset Helps You Use Time Better

Having a growth mindset is like having a secret superpower when it comes to time management. Here's how it helps:

You embrace challenges: When you face something difficult, like a big project or a tough exam, a growth mindset helps you see it as an opportunity to learn rather than something to avoid. This means you're more likely to put in the effort and work through it, even when it's hard.

You don't give up easily: People with a growth mindset are more persistent. If they don't get something right the first time, they try again. They understand that mistakes are part of learning. This means they don't waste time feeling frustrated or giving up—they keep going until they get it right.

You take responsibility for your time: With a growth mindset, you believe you have control over your abilities and your time. If something goes wrong, instead of blaming others or making excuses, you look at what you can do to improve. This helps you take charge of your time and make better decisions about how to spend it.

3. How a Fixed Mindset Holds You Back

On the other hand, a fixed mindset can waste a lot of time. Here's how it can affect your time management:

You avoid challenges: If you believe you're not good at something, you might avoid trying it altogether. This means you're not giving yourself the chance to grow or improve, which wastes your potential and time.

You get stuck in failure: When you have a fixed mindset, failure feels like the end of the road instead of a learning opportunity. If you don't succeed at something, you might give up and waste time feeling defeated instead of learning from your mistakes and moving forward.

You believe time is limited: People with a fixed mindset often think that their abilities are fixed. This can lead them to believe they don't have enough time to improve. They might feel like they've already reached their limit and that they can't achieve more, which can make them give up on their goals.

4. Changing Your Mindset

The good news is that you can change your mindset! Here are a few ways to develop a growth mindset and make the most of your time:

Recognize your thoughts: The first step is to pay attention to how you think about yourself and your time. Are you thinking, "I'm not good enough," or "I'll never finish this on time"? If you catch yourself thinking this way, challenge those thoughts. Instead, say, "I can get better with practice," or "I can find a way to make this work."

Celebrate progress, not perfection: Instead of focusing on being perfect, focus on the progress you're making. Every small step forward is a win! This shift in thinking helps you stay motivated and use your time to make steady improvements.

Learn from failure: If something goes wrong or you don't meet your goals, don't see it as a failure. Instead, think about what you can learn from the experience. Ask yourself, "What can I do differently next time?" This will help you use your time more wisely in the future.

Surround yourself with positivity: The people around you can also affect your mindset. Try to spend time with people who encourage you to grow, challenge you to do better, and celebrate your successes.

5. The Power of Positive Thinking

Your thoughts have a powerful impact on how you use your time. Positive thinking can help you stay focused, motivated, and ready to tackle challenges. Instead of thinking, "I don't have enough time," try thinking, "I have time to work on what matters most." Positive thinking doesn't mean ignoring problems, but it helps you focus on solutions and move forward.

6. Staying Motivated and Productive with the Right Mindset

A growth mindset can also help you stay motivated and productive. When you believe that your effort leads to improvement, you're more likely to stay focused on your goals, even when things get tough. Here's how to stay motivated:

Break big tasks into small steps: Big tasks can feel overwhelming, but if you break them into smaller, manageable steps, they feel more achievable. This makes it easier to stay on track and motivated to keep going.

Set small, achievable goals: Set goals that are realistic and can be accomplished in a short amount of time. Each time you achieve a goal, you'll feel more motivated to keep going.

Focus on the process, not just the outcome: Enjoy the journey, not just the result. If you focus on doing your best and learning along the way, you'll be more productive and make the most of your time.

Closing Thoughts

Your mindset shapes how you use your time. If you believe in your ability to grow, learn, and improve, you'll find that you can make the most of every moment. With a growth mindset, you can face challenges, stay motivated, and make better decisions about how to use your time. So, start thinking positively, embrace your ability to improve, and watch how your time management skills grow!

Exercise

Think about a task or goal that feels challenging to you. What are your thoughts about it? Do you have a fixed mindset, like "I'll never be good at this," or a growth mindset, like "I can improve with practice"? Write down how you can change your thoughts to focus on growth and improvement. Also, think of one small step you can take today to move closer to that goal.

Afterword

As I come to the end of this book, I want to leave you with one final thought: time is the most valuable thing we have. It's something that constantly slips away, often without us even noticing. But the truth is, how we spend our time shapes everything—our happiness, our relationships, and even the person we become.

Writing this book has been a journey in itself, one of realizing just how much we take time for granted. I've learned, through reflection and experience, that it's not about having more time, but about making the time we do have truly matter.

It's easy to get caught up in the rush of life, but if there's anything I hope you take away from these pages, it's that every moment counts. Time isn't something that waits for you—it's something you make the most of, moment by moment.

So, as you go forward, I encourage you to think about how you're spending your time. Is it adding value to your life? Is it aligned with what truly matters to you? The answers may not always be easy, but taking the time to ask yourself these questions can make all the difference.

Thank you for sharing this time with me. I hope these words have inspired you to reflect, to pause, and to make your time count in ways that truly matter to you.

- Aaleyah Rahmani

TWO PLAYS

FAMAGUSTA AND BRITISH TELECOM

Aditya Sondhi

ISBN 979-8-89906-968-0